MY LIFE CONTRACT

90-Day Program

for Prioritizing Goals,

Staying on Track,

Keeping Focused, and

Getting Results

JOEL FOTINOS

Foreword by Laura Berman Fortgang

HAMPTON ROADS

Cover design by Jim Warner
Interior designed by Frame25 Productions

Hampton Roads Publishing Company, Inc.
Charlottesville, VA 22906
Distributed by Red Wheel/Weiser, LLC
www.redwheelweiser.com

Sign up for our newsletter and special offers by going to *www.redwheelweiser.com/newsletter/.*

ISBN: 978-1-57174-723-5

Library of Congress Cataloging-in-Publication Data available upon request

Printed in the United States of America.
EBM

10 9 8 7 6 5 4 3 2 1

For my beloved Team Family, as always . . .

CONTENTS

The price of anything is the amount of life you exchange for it.
—Henry David Thoreau

Energy follows action.
—Joel Fotinos

There is a place that you are to fill that no one else can,
and something you are to do which no one else can do.
—Florence Scovel Shinn

We are what we repeatedly do.
Excellence, then, is not an act, but a habit.
—Aristotle

FOREWORD

I love contracts and clear agreements. Every time I've gone without one, it's resulted in conflicts, misunderstandings, or disappointments. It's no wonder I'm crazy about the concept contained here in *My Life Contract*. It makes complete sense. We don't usually do business without a contract, so why set goals for ourselves without one? A contract means we're serious!

Even more intriguing is the suggestion herein that when we make a life contract, we are also making a contract with God or the Universe or whatever term you might use for the unseen forces that somehow organize our existence. In essence, we are announcing a partnership with the Universe: "I'll do my part, you do yours!"

Contracts provide us with built-in accountability. We want to keep our word to ourselves and to others. Contracts formalize our intent to keep impeccably to our word. In my role as a personal coach for more than twenty years, I've held open the space for people to keep their word to themselves. It's not the zenith of my skill set, but it's part of the magic that happens when we are determined to change once and for all.

As Joel mentions, it's okay to make the pieces of our goal bite-sized so we can achieve each one and stay accountable to ourselves to complete the whole. It's often the largesse of our ambition that keeps us paralyzed or causes us to give up too soon. And if that describes you, you have picked up the right book. The tool that Joel has created here is truly brilliant. It's simple, clear, and so practical that if you use it daily, you'll be surprised at how very powerful you are. Joel's system will work its magic on you, and you'll be amazed at what you are capable of when you do your part and surrender the two parts that are *not* yours to worry about. (No spoilers here, read the book!)

You may have heard it said that if you make a step toward what you want, divine providence will follow. I can confidently confirm that I have seen this notion at work hundreds of times. When clients finally decide to take action on something they've not thought possible before, it is not uncommon, in my experience, to see some pretty miraculous things happen. It's as if their "luck" is suddenly multiplied, intensified, and accelerated by their commitment to move toward something that unifies them with their deepest core self. A profound desire with no room for doubt + a serious demonstration of this belief through definitive action = positive outcome.

If you don't believe this can work for you, it won't. You'll be right.

If you abandon yourself to the process laid out for you in this book, something will result that you'll be happy with.

Believe, trust, and act. But first, READ.

Enjoy.

—Laura Berman Fortgang
Pioneer in the personal coaching field and author of *Living Your Best Life* and
Now What?: 90 Days to a New Life Direction

INTRODUCTION

Welcome to your Contract with Life. This is the beginning of an incredible success story—yours!

Are you someone who wants more financial prosperity in your life? Or perhaps greater health? More love? Perhaps your goal is to deepen spiritually? Whatever has drawn you to this book, you will find ideas and actions that will bring you to your goals and dreams—or even to surpass them.

How do I know? Not only have the ideas in this book worked for me, I've seen them work for countless people who have taken my classes and workshops over the years. I've seen people apply them to love, money, happiness, joy, health, spiritual understanding, creative expression, building a successful business, and so much more. The reasons we bring to bear are as individual as we are, but the ideas work the same no matter what the goal.

Here in this introduction, you are going to get an overview of what a Life Contract is and why it is important to discover one and use it. In part one, we will delve into learning about the Life Contract, and in part two, we actually put the Life Contract into practice. Part three contains additional information, including the Life Purpose Questionnaire, instructions for forming a Master Mind partnership or group, and additional resources.

Each section of this book is designed to inspire and motivate you to take action in your life.

How I Discovered the Life Contract

Have you ever wanted to find a magical formula that would help you to discover how to have what you desire in life? How to get more money, more love, more meaning? And have you read a bunch of books, gone to seminars, and watched *Oprah* religiously for years trying to figure out that formula?

I have.

It took some time, but I did find the formula that worked for me. For more than twenty years, I read thousands of self-help and spiritual books, attended hundreds of lectures, took countless classes, and studied every religion and school of psychology that I could. I kept looking for what would help me move forward in life, instead of feeling stuck and small and broke and insignificant. It was a mission for me to see which of the self-help programs, authors, teachers, or gurus held "the answer." Was it Tony Robbins? Weight Watchers? AA? A new health supplement? The new channeled material everyone was talking about? That exercise program I saw on the late-night infomercial? *Think and Grow Rich*? I explored everything I could get my hands on.

Let me have done all of that work for you. And now, I can share the results of what I discovered.

I eventually figured something out that should save you the trouble of repeating my quest. Underneath all of those books, those classes, those teachings from the most successful authors was a simple formula. Once I figured it out, I saw the formula in every book or lecture I came across. And even now, all these years later, I still see this formula everywhere. But no one has singled it out so that it can be used by anyone for anything.

Once I had the formula, I immediately put it to work. At the time, I was heavily in debt, without a significant other, depressed, and in a job that felt like it had no future. Can you relate to any of that? It was a dark time, and it was made worse by a feeling that life was passing me by, that I was somehow missing out on something that other people seemed to know about, but I was excluded from. I had very little joy in my life.

Knowing how the formula works literally saved me. It gave me a clear map to all I wanted in life. And then it took me further. I'll explain all of this in the next few chapters, but for here, let me say that this map, this formula, this process became my ticket to the life I had always imagined but didn't really believe would come about. It took the "magic" out of getting what I wanted and let me know what was mine to do and what I should let go of. In short, it was a life "master class," and I continue to use it to this day.

Eventually, though, as I began to use the formula and fine-tune my experience of it, I came to think of it as a contract—My Life Contract. Then I began teaching the Life Contract principles and saw how powerfully they transformed other lives as well. It is all so clear and simple, nearly everyone is able to grasp the concepts and begin applying them immediately.

What I Mean by "Life"

This book combines spiritual principles with concepts from psychology, science, and art. Each of those disciplines has a different vernacular, at times saying similar things with distinctive terminology. Certain word choices carry more baggage than others, and one of those words is "God." I tend not to reference it because so many people have such varied and strong associations with "God." My own conception has changed over the years as well from a male, bearded figure who lives somewhere in the heavens (which I believed as a child, much as I believed in Santa Claus) to something that is far less finite but much more powerful.

I have shifted over time to using the word "Life" (with a capital "L") to mean that universal force or power that has created all living beings. Life, for me, means that "something beyond" that is bigger than us, that is nameless, infinite, and indefinable. It is the Tao, the One Mind, the Creator. (When I use "life," then I'm speaking about our own individual lives.)

You can feel free to think in terms of whatever you want to mean a supreme being or intelligent force. Or, if you'd rather, consider the word "Life" in more secular terms, such as simply that unknowable *something* that we all can feel. That's okay as well.

It doesn't matter what you call it; just know that here I'm going to call it Life.

Engage in Your Own Life

In the following pages, you'll find the instructions about the Life Contract as well as a ninety-day program to help you move into action. But let me say something before you go any further. While these steps are the ones I discovered to move me from where I was to where I wanted to be, *I made my Life Contract my top priority.*

The pain in my life had gotten to the point that I was willing to do whatever it took to move forward.

My wish for you if you are in pain in your life, or if you are looking for a map to your life purpose, is that you make your Life Contract *your* priority. The more you do, the faster your desires will become a reality. Give yourself the gift of being invested in this journey, of being consistent and wanting to give the best of yourself to this process. As the saying goes, halfhearted measures avail nothing. You must put your whole heart and soul into your journey.

If you don't recall anything more from this introduction than this, please remember the following: *Once you actively engage in your own life, then Life will engage with you.* The point of these steps is not to sit back and have Life bring you what you want; it's to have you become so engaged in your own success that Life can't help but bring you what you want—and more. You are about to become an active participant in your own healing. One of my life truths has been *If you want more, you must first become more.* This book is the map to becoming more.

Another important thing I discovered in creating a Life Contract for myself, as well as having taught this process for more than a decade to thousands of others, is that your results are your own responsibility. You get to be an active participant in your own Contract with Life.

One of my base beliefs is that Life always wants more for us than we want for ourselves. We often seem to ask for so little. We take our meager crumbs and say "thank you" while inwardly resenting our small portion or that others seem to receive more. But that isn't Life's choice, that's usually our own. We sometimes:

- Ask for too little
- Don't believe we deserve anything
- Begrudge others having more than ourselves
- Want to stay comfortable more than we want to grow
- Sabotage our own efforts
- Don't stay focused
- Procrastinate

Do any of these sound familiar? If you can relate to one or more of them, this book is for you.

Energy Follows Action

So, keep turning the pages and start your journey. What's the first step? I've learned that *energy follows action*. We want to be inspired *before* we move. We want to have enough money or enough energy or enough time *before* we commit to change. But life doesn't work that way. We have to take action first, putting into motion an entire chain of events that will in turn create our life.

Have you ever heard the saying, "If you want something done, don't give it to someone with a lot of time on their hands, give it to someone busy"? What that means is that people who are already in motion often can get more things done, faster, than people who are stationary.

We are all so good at waiting! Many times I will hear people say, "I will take action, but I'm waiting for the time to be right first." That sounds reasonable, doesn't it? But this is actually a delay tactic. We find ways to delay our own good outcomes by staying in the same place, day after day, year after year.

Isaac Newton, the seventeenth-century physicist, famously taught that an object at rest will stay at rest, while an object in motion will continue to move. This book and its process are designed to get you moving, so that the motion you create generates an even greater momentum. Just reading this book isn't action: it's a good start, but no substitute for the real thing. The activities here will ask you to get clear about what you want, and then begin taking steps toward it. You may resist a bit at first, but once you start moving, there will be no stopping you!

What You Focus On Grows

It's important to realize that the way you look at your life will determine your experience of life. For instance, those with a positive outlook tend to have a more positive experience of a situation than those with a negative outlook, and they will also have a more positive outcome.

A number of years ago, I worked with two women who both were going through divorces. They had similar life situations—about the same age, about the same economic background, no children, and husbands who had cheated on them—but their response to their divorces couldn't have been more different. The first woman kept saying over and over that the divorce was the worst thing that had ever happened to her, that it was a disaster, she wasn't sure how she could move forward, and she was filled with rage toward her husband. The second woman had many of the same feelings of anger and disappointment about her divorce, but her outlook seemed different. She kept saying over and over that she was going to use this opportunity to reinvent her life, was grateful for all this had given and taught her, and was going to find a better man to marry next time.

I'm not minimizing the experience these women went through, but I don't want to over-maximize it, either. It's educational to see how one person can choose to see an experience positively, which sets up a positive outcome, and the other can see it so negatively, which sets up a negative outcome. Which woman do you think has learned the lessons from that first marriage and gone on to live life fully and find love again? And which woman do you think is still talking about the husband who betrayed her and is still angry and stuck?

"But this situation is different, my situation is *really* bad . . ." I hear frequently from the people I coach (and I've certainly said that to myself over the years). We almost want our situation to be the one that is the exception to Life's laws, so that we can feel justified in our disappointment or victimhood. That way, our being stuck or poor, or whatever, will be someone else's fault.

Now, think for a moment about those people whom you admire, those people who have achieved love or success or wealth or happiness. When you talk with those people or see them on television, do you hear them wallow in the negatives of life? Is anything holding them back? No, you always hear them discuss how they overcame obstacles and went on toward what they wanted in life by focusing on it every day. They put their attention on their goal, not their past. They let their future dreams and goals determine their present actions and beliefs, rather than relying on the past and what hasn't worked before. You can, too, and this book will help.

Now It's Your Turn

Are you ready? Are you excited to finally move forward in your life?

Sometimes when I ask people this, they give me a long list of all the reasons why they aren't ready or why the conditions in their life aren't right for change or why their past is holding them back—or a million other excuses. They can tell me in great detail why they don't have what they want and why it probably won't happen for them now. We love our stories of limitation and tell them brilliantly! As Richard Bach wrote in his classic book *Illusions*: "Argue your limitations, and sure enough, they're yours."

When I press them further, they'll often say something along the lines of "you don't know me, and you don't know why I can't commit to something right now."

That's when I look them right in the eye and calmly but firmly tell them, "Yes, I do know you, but I don't think that *you* know YOU! You've just spent the last several minutes telling me about all of your limitations. I don't think you realize how strong you are, how much Life wants you to succeed, how many people are willing to help you. I see limitless potential in you, and I see that you are ready now. There is no other time! What are you waiting for?"

I say the same thing to you now. Don't wait one more moment to live your life fully! You were not created to be small and live a tepid, mediocre life. You were not created by accident. You are here to grow and live fully and love gloriously. You are here to experience all that Life has to offer and to help others do the same. Wherever you are in your life, *now* is the perfect time to move forward. You have exactly the right tools to succeed. Life is ready to help.

Take a deep breath, and then say out loud: I AM READY TO LIVE THE LIFE I LOVE! And now, turn the page, and begin the journey . . .

PART ONE

UNDERSTANDING THE LIFE CONTRACT

Your Contract with Life

When you want a change in your life of any kind and decide you want to do something about it, you are entering into what I call a Contract with Life. You are partnering with the Divine to create whatever it is you desire.

Just as in any contract, there are certain requirements expected of both parties. For example, if I were to sign a contract with someone to build a house, my part of the contract might include paying for materials and labor as well as supplying detailed descriptions of what kind of house I want. The builder's part of the contract might include the actual construction of the house, supplying workers, and getting the materials. The contract would most likely include deadlines when certain parts of the house must be done: On January 1, the foundation must be set and the wooden structure completed. By March 1, all the drywall up and a roof put on. By June 1, the house is completed.

And it is the same with our Life Contract.

I've found that in our Life Contract, we have six main responsibilities, and Life has two main responsibilities.

Life Contract Map

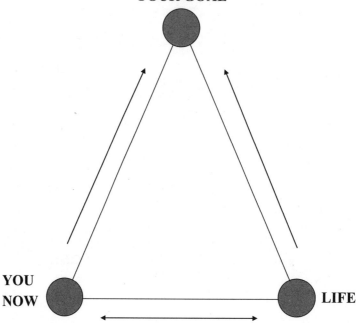

YOUR GOAL

YOU NOW

LIFE

Your Contractual Responsibilities

1. Get Clear about Where You Are Now

2. Get Clear about What You Want

3. Make a Decision

4. Take Action Immediately

5. C&P: Be Consistent and Persistent

6. Strive for Excellence

Life's Contractual Responsibilities

1. How

2. When

Our Contractual Tasks

Let's begin with *our* six responsibilities in the Life Contract.

1. Get Clear about Where You Are

In order to move to where we want to be in life, we must first have a good sense of where we are. I'm not talking about the location of your house or what city you live in. What I mean is that you must have a real sense of where you stand in the area or areas of your life that you want to change and grow. This is one of those "get real" times, where you don't sugarcoat or overdramatize your position.

For example, if you want more money and greater financial prosperity, the first step would be to understand exactly what your finances look like now. When people mention in my classes that they want more money and I ask them how much money they have, or how much debt they are carrying, they often can't tell me. How can Life help you when you aren't clear about your own situation?

Similarly, if you wanted to lose weight, you would first need to know how much you weigh now. That gives you a starting point. If you want better health, you would need to know what kind of condition you are in. If you want a love relationship, you would want to know the kind of person you are looking for and perhaps explore why you are single (i.e., is there a pattern to your previous relationships, self-esteem issues, etc.). If you want to create a dream career, you would need to know what you like and don't like about the careers you have had and the one you are in now.

This is a time to be totally honest. Look at the whole situation, what you've thought of as the positive and negative parts. If you are a person who has glossed over the negative, this is the time to get real. If you are a person who is overly critical, this is the time to turn off the internal censor and just look at what is.

Either way, whatever you find, just let it be. If you are alarmed by what you see, then reframe what you are looking at as a new beginning, rather than a life sentence.

Here's an example. At one point in my life, the area that needed most of my attention concerned finances. I simply never had enough money to do what I wanted—or, God forbid, repair my car if it needed it. There was no money for my needs, let alone my wants. It was time to get clear about my money situation.

I looked at every bill, every letter, every receipt—and discovered that I was over $57,000 in credit card debt and had twenty-three active credit cards. Well, the credit issuers kept sending me new cards to use, and so I kept using them. I thought, if you can't trust a credit card company, whom can you trust? Clearly I had a lot to learn. I had no savings at all, no 401k plan, and only about thirty dollars in the bank. I got paid every other week, but my paycheck was usually gone within twenty-four hours paying bills and buying some food.

My next step was to get even clearer about where I was, so I visited a financial advisor. While sitting together in his cubicle at the financial institution—a cubicle I clearly remember as having no personal effects at all, no photographs or sentimental knickknacks—this man looked at my whole situation. He punched a bunch of numbers into his calculator, sighed a few times, and asked a couple of questions.

Several agonizing minutes later, he shoved himself away from the desk, swiveled in his chair to face me, and said, "Good news." He then went on to explain that with my current level of debt and salary, he had figured out how long it would take to get out of debt completely. He said, "given your current salary, and including a normal increase as well as a few bonuses over the years, if you do not charge one more cent and follow the pay-off plan that I'll propose to you, as well as begin to create a small savings account, you can get out of debt no later than twenty-three years from now."

Yes, twenty-three *years*.

He thought it was a brilliant plan, and he was smiling, obviously very pleased with himself. I, on the other hand, had a different reaction. My first thought was, "Twenty-three years? I should just kill myself." I wasn't having a real suicidal moment, but his news threw me further into despair. I was in my late twenties, so I would be fifty years old—a lifetime away!—before I would be free of debt.

To discover that I was carrying nearly $60,000 in personal credit card debt was astounding. Yes, I had a number of negative emotions surrounding this situation. Part of me felt humiliated, stupid, and about a thousand other dark feelings.

But I also recognized that this was where I was beginning a new journey. This was my new chapter one in the book of my financial life. I was going to focus on what I wanted to manifest, rather than what I had manifested already.

Ask yourself these things:

- In the area that I want change, I currently am . . .

- What I don't like about this area in my life is . . .

- What I like about this area of my life is . . .

2. Get Clear about What You Want

Now that you are crystal clear about where you are, the next step is to decide where you want to go. Or, to say it another way, now is the time to decide what it is you want in the area that you are focusing on. You can pick one thing or you can do a total overhaul, but my experience has shown that when we focus on one major thing—which can encompass many smaller things—we'll have greater success. Some people make the mistake of trying to set five, ten, or even more goals, and then they wonder why they aren't seeing much forward momentum. However, when we focus on one, two, or no more than three goals, we have more time, energy, and resources to move forward quickly.

Getting clear about what you want can be as easy as choosing something very specific that you need or desire—a new car, getting out of debt, losing weight—or it can be one larger thing—become a millionaire, get healthy, find love—that you can then break down into more concrete goals. You can choose something specific and material or you can go deeper and look for "spiritual meaning" or "surrender to the Divine" as your goal. Either way, the Life Contract will work. When I began that first time, all I wanted was to get out of debt. But later I used the same process to find a life partner, a family, a great career, and deep spiritual development.

If you need help deciding what to do, don't worry. In part two, you'll go through a goal finder exercise that will narrow down what to focus on. And in part three, I've included the powerful Life Purpose Questionnaire.

The point in getting clear is to make sure you know where you are going, what goal you want. It is about choosing something you can commit to. If you are someone who finds it difficult to stay with one thing until it happens, you'll find the Ninety-Day Goal Tracker in part three to be a great tool to keep you on track.

Keep in mind, too, that you can always change your goal as you go forward. As with any contract, you can amend the wording to include a new purpose. But your part of entering into this conscious Life Contract demands that you choose *something* you and Life can now create together.

To continue with the story about my finances, when I got real about where I was in my monetary dealings—when I discovered that I was nearly $60,000 in credit card debt with a meager salary that wasn't covering all my monthly bills, had no savings at all and less than thirty dollars in my checking account, and a financial advisor that I was paying via credit card told me that it would take as long as twenty-three years to get straight—it was time to make some decisions about the outcome that I wished were true for me in the area of money.

When I sat down to decide what I wanted, I remember thinking that I "should" make a goal to be a millionaire with a big house and an expensive car and lots of money in the bank. But at the time, goals like those felt too unreal for me, too "happily ever after."

There in my one-room studio apartment just north of Sausalito, California, I tried to come up with the biggest number that I wanted *but* that also felt like something that could really come true. And in all honesty, the biggest number that came to my mind was zero—just to be completely out of debt. If my best-case scenario was twenty-three years of paying off debt, I knew that I was going to need to make some changes to improve on that.

So I decided that night that my goal would be zero. Zero debt. And that goal felt wonderful. When I thought of that goal, I could breathe again. It made me happy to just imagine it. It was clear enough that there was no ambiguity about what it was that I wanted. It was specific, joyous, and motivating.

Now it's your turn. Pick your goal. Use the same criteria I did in making mine. What would make your life amazing? What would allow you to breathe deeply again? What would you like to be true for you?

Ask yourself these clarifying questions after looking back at your answers from the previous section (on page 5):

- Now that I know where I am and what I don't want, what comes to mind as a good goal to have?

- What would I love in this area of my life?

- What outcome do I want in this particular area?

- What would be the best possible scenario?

(Again, you'll narrow down your goal or goals in the next part of the book, but these questions will get you started.)

3. Make a Decision

Now we come to the moment when you make a decision. I don't mean a casual pick on the level of "where should I go to eat?" or "what movie should I go see?" I'm talking about making a Big Decision—one of those "starting today, my life is going to be different" choices. This is the kind of decision that will generate positive momentum in your life and will require you to make changes and shifts, both internally and in your outer world.

For instance, in my story of financial debt, once I was clear (and in my case, mortified) about where I was and about my goal (zero), it was time to make a decision. Was I going to really move forward and make this come true? Or was I going to continue on living as I had, behind the eight ball, always wondering when my house of cards would come crashing down around me?

I felt into all the pain this situation had caused me and had continued causing me to that very day. I thought about all the things I wanted to do but couldn't because I was so heavily in debt. I thought about how I had been using credit cards to make myself feel better, and began to wonder if there was a different and easier way to do that. I envisioned the person I wanted to be and realized that this debt did not represent that person.

The debt seemed to be standing in the way of what I wanted and who I wanted to be. I didn't realize it then, but just making those connections was a powerful change generator. I wasn't just moving away from something (debt), I was moving toward something as well (my goal).

So it was right then and there that I made my decision—which led me to the next step.

Ask yourself:

- Am I ready to make a change?

- Am I clear about what I want to leave behind and what I want to move toward?

- How will my life feel if I meet this goal?

- Am I willing to do whatever it takes to fulfill my part of this Contract with Life?

4. Take Action Immediately

Have you ever had a great idea and gotten really excited, but then the next day it seems like all of the energy and enthusiasm has dimmed? That's because *the energy for an action is in the present moment.*

I once heard a story of a woman who was looking online for a new job because her current occupation didn't make her happy. In fact, it was downright difficult to get up and go to work each day. She didn't like the job, it didn't pay well, and she felt it was dragging her down. Then she found a posting for a position that sounded perfect for her. As she read about the job, she got excited, because it was both exactly what she wanted to do and her skills and background made her perfect for it. She decided to work on her résumé over the weekend and then send it in.

Did you catch it? Did you catch where she made the mistake?

Instead of taking action immediately, she decided to wait until she "had more time." That's what I call an SDT: a subconscious delay tactic. If the energy for an inspiration or opportunity is in the present moment, then the best time to take action is also in the present moment. Even if you have to write down the ideas or next steps on a napkin in a restaurant, taking some form of action immediately will ensure that you are creating momentum and answering Life's call. But when you delay, you are literally draining the idea of energy.

Well, this woman put off working on her résumé until the weekend, and you know the rest of the story, right? When the weekend came, she didn't "feel like it," so she decided to give it time until she did. She kept telling others how perfect the job was, but then a couple weeks passed. One day, the job posting was gone. Someone else had been hired for her perfect job. How would things have been different for her if she had taken action immediately and sent in a résumé that very day? She might have gotten that new job. Or she might not have, but the experience would have made her realize how dissatisfied she was and sparked her to find something that suited her better. At the very least, taking action immediately would have created forward movement.

Here are some common ways we delay our good:

- Waiting until we have more time

- Waiting until we have more money

- Waiting until we feel like it

- Waiting until the time is right

- Waiting until the weekend

- Waiting until we have more free time

- Waiting until we get approval from a family member or friend

- Waiting until the house is clean

- Waiting until the car is fixed

- Waiting until we are at the computer

For me, once I made my decision, I knew that I needed to take action immediately before I chickened out and got into even worse debt. The action that I took was to immediately gather up all twenty-three of my active credit cards, a pair of scissors, and a glass of wine for courage. I cut up each of the cards, put them all into a bag, and walked them out to the apartment complex's big trash bin. Then I went back to my apartment and considered what to do next.

It was such a big step that I'm only mildly embarrassed to tell you that I then went back outside to the trash bin, got that plastic bag, went back to my apartment, reassembled all twenty-three cards, and then taped the pieces for each card onto notebook paper, and put those pages into a three-ring binder (which I still have to this day, to remind me of my commitment). That's how strong my dependence on those credit cards was.

I took the action step. Sure, part of me felt miserable and scared, and yet part of me—some very small part of me—felt excited. It felt like I had just taken the first step on a new journey.

When we take action, it doesn't have to be a huge thing, and it doesn't have to be a tiny thing. It needs to be the right thing. The action should feel like the most meaningful step relating to your goal. To become debt-free was my main idea, getting to zero was my goal, and cutting up my credit cards was my action that first day.

Students in my classes have chosen many different first moves. One woman who was looking for a love match decided to sign up for two online dating services that very day as her immediate step. Was that the only action she would take? Of course not, but we all need to start somewhere.

Another student decided he was going to sign up for Weight Watchers online right away and not wait until the next meeting in his area, which was several days away. Still another contacted a real estate agent to discuss selling her home and looking for a new one—she literally made the call right there on a break during the class. Someone else spent a half hour after class beginning the novel he wanted to write.

If you are unclear about what action to take now, I've included a very powerful exercise in part three, called "Sitting for Ideas." Try this technique, and see what comes up.

Get moving! Just start now!

Ask yourself:

- What is the right action for me to take today?

- Is this action too small? Too big? Or does it feel just right?

- What feelings does taking this action bring up for me?

- Am I willing to do it anyway?

5. C&P: Be Consistent and Persistent

Okay, you've defined what you want, made the decision to go for it, and taken immediate action. Now comes the part that derails most people. I call it C&P, which stands for being "consistent and persistent." Being consistent means that you take action every single day toward what it is that you want. Being persistent means you take action especially on those days when you don't want to.

Let's face it, there will be times you want to sleep in and just avoid doing what you know is the right thing to do. There will be moments when your inner resistance will rear its ugly head in the form of procrastination, boredom, anger, disinterest, drama, or something else that will try to get you off track. Here are some common ways that resistance shows up to try to derail our progress:

- Procrastination

- A cold or flu

- Anger

- Drama with friend or family member

- Drama at work

- Avoidance

- Moodiness

- Preoccupation with television, the Internet, etc.

- A sudden desire to do *anything* but the task at hand

Our subconscious mind likes to stay within a certain comfort zone we have created over the years—not too much discomfort and not too much pleasure. Just like the thermostat in your house, if the gauge goes one degree lower than your comfort zone, your subconscious will kick into action and galvanize you to elevate your mood, but just until you get back into your comfort zone. Then the inner thermostat turns off again. Similarly, if the gauge goes one degree higher than the ceiling of your comfort zone's acceptable happiness level, your subconscious will create some distraction or mood or drama that will bring you right back down into that comfortable place again.

Why is this important to know? Because when we are aware that our subconscious does this, we can override the inner thermostat so we can experience greater levels of joy, happiness, and success. If you know that once you begin any elevating journey, you will be tempted to participate in one of the many ways your subconscious will try to bring you back down, then you can make different choices.

Forewarned is forearmed. So consider this your warning. Once you know your subconscious's game, it's almost comical (if it weren't so painful) to see how desperate it is to pull you back to the lower level.

This is why C&P is the key to your part of the contract. When you make that strong commitment and take action every day, then you are creating a new experience, a new "normal," a new comfort zone.

My experience with my debt drove this deeply home to me. Once I made the decision to change, get out of debt, and cut up my credit cards, I began the real journey. Every day I needed to remind myself that I was on a journey, that I had committed myself to this Life Contract, and that the more action I took that day, the more results I would see.

Like compound interest which builds upon itself, it didn't take long before I saw early results. Within a couple of months, my debt total began going down.

However, I was tempted every which way by my subconscious to get off track and go back to my old ways. I would develop a sudden desire for something that I could only afford by using a credit card. A business trip would come up where I rationalized that I needed to use a credit card. I would go out to dinner with friends and not have enough cash to pay my portion of the bill, so instead of using a cash machine, I would want to use my credit card.

At one point, I went into a deep depression that lasted for months. As I journaled through it, what I came to understand is that the old part of me—that part of me who wanted to go back to my "usual" behavior—was dying. A new "me" was being created, and the depression was part of that experience. Of course, the more depressed I became, the more I wanted to use my credit cards. But what helped me the most to stay on track is that I had created a goal that was so exciting that I was willing to walk through this temporary difficulty to come out on the other side.

C&P is the cornerstone of every journey to a new experience. To lose weight, you must commit yourself daily to eat correctly and exercise. To stay sober, you must commit yourself daily to not use the substance you are addicted to. To get out of debt, I needed to commit myself daily to not use credit cards and to behave responsibly with money. To find the love of your life, you must remind yourself daily that you are the love of your life and treat yourself accordingly.

While there are difficult days ahead, and you will need the persistence to continue with your part of the contract, you will also find that there are wonderful days ahead as well. Every time I reached a new goal in my journey out of debt, it would feel amazing. I often would pause and find a small free or inexpensive way to reward myself when I reached a new goal.

If you find yourself tempted to break your part of the contract through a lure of any kind or a delay tactic, say this to yourself:

C&P is the way to the life I want. I recommit myself here and now!

By the way, there are some people who attend my longer twelve- or fourteen-week classes and struggle to stay the course. I always let people know that is normal, but to carry on. One way I have found to remain consistent and persistent is to share this experience with another person who has signed a Contract with Life for a desire or dream. See part three for more information about traveling this journey with someone else in the section about creating a Master Mind partnership.
Ask yourself:

- What are the ways I tend to derail myself from experiencing more joy, happiness, and success?

- How can I find ways to stay committed each and every day?

- Is there someone I can choose to help me stay accountable to during this experience?

- Do I want my goal or dream or desire enough to get through the resistance?

- If not, do I need to up my goal so it is even more desirable?

6. Strive for Excellence

There is a Buddhist saying that I love: "The way you do anything is the way you do everything." What that means is that if you enter into your Contract with Life with enthusiasm, commitment, willingness, and positivity, then you will more likely get better results than someone who enters into theirs with a halfhearted or tepid commitment. I've noticed that people who want to put in minimal effort and receive maximum results are usually disappointed and drop out fairly quickly. Those are the people who want this to be like magic, where they don't have to do much but will get everything. But the Life Contract doesn't operate that way. It requires us to change and grow and be responsible for our part toward getting what it is we desire. As I often say:

In order to have more, you must become more.

That makes sense, right? You can't be the same person and yet get different results. When I write that down so plainly, it makes complete sense. However, that is exactly what many of us do. We say we want our life to change . . . as long as our life doesn't actually change. With money, for instance, we say we want more, but unless we adapt our consciousness about money and our actions with money, we can't have anything but the same experience with money.

I remember that early in my journey out of debt, I would often think, "If only someone would just give me a check for $57,000, then I could pay off my debt and my life will be great again." However, what I learned through the longer process—and studies on human behavior seem to support this—is that if someone had given me that check for $57,000, not only would I get back into debt again, but more likely even deeper debt.

This is why studies show that the majority of lottery winners who receive large amounts of money end up without the money and in even worse shape than before they won it within a very short period of time. *They* didn't change, just their circumstances, so their circumstances were pulled right back to where their consciousness was.

Here's another example. Shortly after I eventually got out of debt (more on that later), I decided to help a friend of mine get out of debt. By then, I had amassed a small savings account of several thousand dollars. My friend was in around $10,000 worth of debt and struggling. She kept saying that if only her debt were gone, her life would be good. Sound familiar? I had said those very words myself!

Even though she hadn't asked me for any money, I knew how stifling debt could feel, and so I decided to give her the $10,000. I even went so far as to get it in cash and hide it in her apartment so that she would be surprised to find it. When she came across it, she cried and called me, saying she was so grateful and would pay off her entire debt and begin life anew. It felt great to help her, and when she sent off her bills in the mail and became debt-free, we went out for a wonderful dinner to celebrate.

Fast-forward twelve months. Not only was she back in debt, but she owed $15,000. She felt awful and eventually declared bankruptcy. I don't begrudge her the money I had shared with her in the slightest. Why? Because it was a valuable lesson that I learned, and it only cost me $10,000 to learn it! What was it? That in order for us to experience something new in our lives, we must adapt and grow and become new.

My friend didn't change her consciousness or behavior, and her results showed it. I've certainly had that happen in my life before, but this experience taught me that we must commit ourselves to doing whatever it takes in order to stay focused on our new goal. (By the way, a quick update about this friend: a few years later she did eventually "get it" and is now using the ideas in this book and prospering in her life.)

Half-measures avail nothing. I heard this in a recovery group, and it has stuck with me in every endeavor I have undertaken. When we enter into our contract with a halfhearted commitment and effort, we will not even get half of the results we want. We usually end up right back where we started or worse. However, when we commit to the Life Contract and decide that we will give it our best shot, we will experience something beyond where we've ever been before.

Striving for excellence doesn't mean that we are striving for perfection. Perfection can be a false goal that keeps us from experiencing our good. I like the word "excellence" more than "perfection" because excellence means giving the best I can at any given moment versus some ideal that I might never reach. Excellence is a mind-set, whereas perfection, to me, is an external value.

It feels good to give our best. We don't have to give more than our best, but deciding that we won't give less provides us with confidence and self-esteem, and those in turn will yield better results.

In my own experience of getting out of debt, I could see better results those weeks and months that I was more committed than those weeks or months when I was less diligent. The more I strove to go forward as excellently as I could, the more (and the faster) I moved forward.

Give yourself the gift of committing to think, believe, and act with as much excellence as you can each day.

What does excellence look like?

- Being enthusiastic

- Not stopping, even though you might feel like it

- Believing more in your dream or goal than in the circumstances that you might currently see

- Making the best choices you can in any given situation

- Surrounding yourself with positive people who believe the best in you

- Wanting the positive change more than you want the status quo

Ask yourself:

- How committed am I to my goal or dream?

- Does my level of commitment match the results I want to see?

- What is required of me to do my best today?

Now you know our six main responsibilities in our Contract with Life. It's time to look at Life's side of the contract. Life has two main responsibilities, both of which we wish were in our part of the contract . . .

Life's Contractual Obligations

Life's #1: How

Whether we realize it or not, the thing we all most wish we could control in our Life Contract is "how." As in:

- How is what I want going to come to me?

- How can Life bring me exactly what I want, exactly when I want?

- How can this work, when I can't see the mechanism?

What I believe is that when we focus on our part of the Life Contract, we become engaged in our life, and that allows Life to become engaged with us. As we do our part, Life is then free to find the ways and means to help us to our goals and dreams. But when we try to micromanage Life's part, we aren't staying on our side of the contract.

We often want to know "how" our goal or our dream will come true for us before we embark on getting there. In other words, we want a guarantee that if we take action toward what we want, it is going to show up exactly as we want it and in the exact time frame we wish.

What I hear often in classes is that someone will say they don't want to risk moving toward their dream or their goal because they cannot see how it could ever come true. The "how" is the thing that stops us cold. If we can't see how it is going to come, then we believe that it won't.

For instance, a woman in one of my classes, whom I'll call Jane, said that she wanted to manifest $25,000, which she was going to use to pay off bills. At just over eighty years of age, Jane said that she wanted to have a freer financial life, and $25,000 would be just enough for her to stop worrying and relax about money.

However, Jane said she knew she wasn't going to get the $25,000 because she "couldn't see how the Universe would send it" to her. She received one retirement check a month, "and they aren't going to send me an extra $25,000 just because I'm a nice lady." Jane didn't have any relatives that she thought would give the money to her, and she wasn't going to go back to work to get the $25,000.

"See," she challenged me, "it is impossible. I want the $25,000, but there is no way I can get it."

Jane made the same mistake that many of us do: she was confusing "source" and "supply." Let's look at these two a little closer. "Source" is Life or God or the Universe or the One—whatever you want to call it. It is that larger creative power that generates all life. "Supply" is the channel by which we receive our good. Source is the well, supply is the bucket.

We often mix the two up. We think that our job (or our monthly check or the government or our parents) is our source. We think our inheritance, our alimony, our royalty, or however else we receive our income, is our source. But the company we work for or the family ties we have or the alternate money generators we rely on are not our source, they are our supply. They can all be a channel through which you receive your good, but they are not the creator of that good.

Jane wanted the $25,000 but could only see the current channel through which she received money: a monthly retirement check. Since she couldn't see any other channel, she believed that no other channel existed for her.

"I want more, but I just don't see how it could come . . ." I hear this same sentiment frequently. Limiting ideas such as: "I want more money, but I'm not sure how my company will give more . . ." or "I want the ideal mate, but I don't know how my boyfriend is going to change into that person . . ."

It's helpful to know that "how" your good comes to you is on Life's side of the contract and not yours. However, I can almost guarantee that you will need to remind yourself of this more than once (even a dozen or a hundred times!) during your journey to your dream. You need to keep letting go of the supply and trust that Life as the source is going to do its part.

Remember Jane, that eighty-year-old student who wanted the $25,000? Well, we discussed this idea of letting Life handle the "how" while she concentrated on her part of the contract. She was resistant. It was just too "out there" for her, and she felt she wanted to know the "how" first before she'd believe. Unfortunately, that's not the way the Life Contract works.

We dialogued back and forth a bit, and eventually I got Jane to open the door of her disbelief just a crack. I asked her if she could just trust this for even a small percentage during class.

Often, if we give Life a tiny opening, that's all it needs to begin making things happen. After a long pause, Jane said she was willing to "go along with it, but only for one week," and she would "only give me a 1 percent willingness" to believe what we were talking about.

"And," she said, "if nothing happens this week, I'm not coming back next week! This is all on you!" I told her that I wasn't her source either, and that if she would honestly commit to giving Life a 1 percent opening, we'd see how Life would show up for her.

The next week rolled around, and as students came into the classroom, I wondered if my toughest one would show up. Just as we were about to close the door and start, in Jane walked. "Since you are here, I assume that means something happened," I said to her.

"Yes," she said, and began to tell us about the week she had had . . .

The morning after the previous week's class, Jane told us, she woke up and wanted to call the whole "Life Contract" philosophy hogwash. But she remembered that she had given her word that she would commit 1 percent for one week.

As she sat down to do her Life Contract activities, she had a sudden urge to go to the farmers' market around the corner from her apartment. She told us that she almost didn't go because there was nothing she needed at the market, but she knew from class that when she got a hunch, she should follow through immediately.

So she went to the farmers' market without knowing why. Once she got there, she saw a friend of hers, who happened to be talking to a man Jane had never met before, whom I'll call Bill. Jane's friend introduced her. They all talked for a few minutes, and then Jane's friend had to leave. Since Jane was having a nice time talking with Bill, she told us, she invited Bill to her apartment for a cup of tea to continue talking.

They walked the block or so to Jane's apartment and went inside. As Jane made tea for them, Bill looked around. He made some comments about what a nice apartment she had and then pointed at a trunk and said, "I love that piece!" When Jane saw that he was pointing at the big trunk that was in a corner in her living room, she said, "That old thing! It's been in my family for years, and no one else wanted it so I ended up with it."

Bill explained that he was an interior decorator and had some clients that he was working for, and this trunk would be perfect for the room he was planning for them. "Would you consider selling it?" he asked. "Sure," said Jane. She started to tell him he could have the trunk for fifty bucks if he had movers come and take it away. But before she could say that, he asked, "Would you take $2,500 for it?"

Jane told us that she just stood there, staring at him with her mouth open. Finally she squeaked out a small "yes, sure." He wrote her a check and made arrangements for the pickup later that week. Jane said she literally took the check to the bank the moment he left to make sure it wouldn't bounce. It didn't.

As she told us about this experience, Jane clearly was astounded at how fast and powerfully Life had worked for her. "Still," she said, "I didn't get the whole $25,000 . . ."

"Well," I replied, "you gave Life a 1 percent opening, and it gave you 10 percent return. Maybe if you had given Life a 10 percent opening, Life could have given you a 100 percent return on your faith!"

Life found a perfect channel to bring Jane's good to her, using an old item that Jane didn't even like or know had value.

What do you think would have happened if Jane had not followed through on that original hunch while she was doing her Life Contract work, which represented her 1 percent faith, and decided not to go to the farmers' market?

Jane finished the class, continued the Life Contract work, and ended up with more than the $25,000 she had originally asked for. She also self-published a novel and began creating art. She engaged in her life, kept up her part of the Life Contract, and Life did its part as well by providing the "how."

As you go through your Life Contract experience, you will probably find yourself getting stuck a number of times, trying to figure out "how" Life is going to give you your good. When you do, gently remind yourself that "how" isn't your responsibility, and then leave that up to Life.

Life's #2: When

If Life is responsible for "how" we receive our good, it is also responsible for "when" it comes to us. But there are a couple of layers to discuss in relation to the "when."

Many self-help books will tell us that not only do we need to get clear about what we want, but we also need to get clear about when we want it. "Set a deadline," many of those books and teachers tell us. Napoleon Hill, in his famous success classic *Think and Grow Rich*, writes "set a Definite Date" when you want your goal to be realized.

Setting a deadline for our goal is a correct thing to do. We do need to set deadlines for our goals, and "Definite Dates" of when we want our good to be realized. However, we must not be held hostage to those deadlines. As the eighties rock band 38 Special once sang, "hold on loosely, but don't let go." That's how we should hold deadlines: loosely.

See, the kind of deadlines that those self-help authors and books tell us about serve not to tell Life "when" to get us our goal, but rather to keep *us* focused and motivated in moving forward. The deadline isn't for Life, it's for us!

The real "when" comes from Life, based on our actions. The more we focus on our part of the Life Contract, the clearer the way is for Life to bring us our goal. If we are tepid or inconsistent or moving slowly, then Life has no choice but to mirror that effort. If we are laser-focused, wholehearted, and open to all of the promptings that we get from Life along the way, the more Life will mirror that effort.

Remember my experience with the financial advisor telling me it would take twenty-three years to get out of debt in a best-case scenario? And remember how that information initially depressed me? It also motivated me to stay the course and move toward my goal each and every day. I set my Life Contract as my main priority and remembered to do my part every day.

And did I set a deadline for getting out of debt? Yes, and it certainly wasn't twenty-three years! I had decided that I wanted out in five years. I didn't know "how" I was going to do it, but I knew that it was going to be my mission to do everything that I could—my part of the Life Contract—to make this happen.

You might be curious whether I reached my goal, and if so, how long it actually took me . . .

I did become debt-free. And it didn't take twenty-three years; it didn't even take five. I ended up paying off all of my debt, on my own (without the help of family or loans), in about three and a half years!

Life matched my excitement, passion, and commitment. A series of events helped me to move out of debt faster than I ever dreamed—and in ways I never could have predicted. Raises, a new higher-paying job, and a series of fun money-raising activities all combined to help me reach my goal. As my prosperity consciousness grew, so did the ways that Life brought me more and more prosperity.

One thing that helped was that I recognized that the Life Contract is like a game. The more fun I had with this game, the faster the results came. I made it a fun challenge to think of as many ways as possible to make money and save money in any given month. One month I sold a bunch of items I no longer wanted on eBay.

Another month I held an in-apartment rummage sale just for my friends. I saved money creatively, including trying to find every free activity I could. As a result, I went to "free days" at respected museums, saw free movies in public parks, and even attended free admission days at the skating rink at Rockefeller Plaza. My gratitude for each and every one of these activities created a grateful heart, and Life rushed in to give me more good.

At one point, I decided to accept everything that was offered to me with love. That month a number of friends spontaneously offered to take me to dinner, or a colleague at work gave me some beautiful clothes that no longer fit him (but fit me perfectly), and I received a surprise check in the mail from a utility company that said I had overpaid and was refunding the difference. When I parked, I looked for spaces that had meters with time still running.

I received it all with joy, and I learned a valuable lesson: There is so much abundance in the world, and when I was attuned to receive it, I began to see it everywhere. I was so busy enjoying all of the free things that I found that I never once felt deprived or poor. I felt prosperous!

Treating this serious matter of huge debt with a light hand and with enjoyment all conspired to speed up my process and bring me quickly to my goal.

However, I have had the opposite experience as well, where the goal was only attained later than my own loose deadline. Once, I was using the Life Contract for a sum of money I wanted in order to make a major purchase. The deadline I had loosely given myself was three months.

Three months came and went, and my goal was seemingly nowhere in sight. Rather than give up in despair, I remembered that I was holding my deadline loosely, and that Life was in charge of "when" my goal would manifest. I stayed focused on the goal and kept doing my part of the Life Contract responsibilities with joy and anticipation.

One day, the phone rang. I answered it and was surprised that it was a leader of a nonprofit in the same city I lived in. Would I be willing to come and teach a course on prosperity consciousness to their group, this leader asked? Sure, I replied, and then we began to talk about the details. When the subject turned to compensation, this leader stated that they would be willing to give me a percentage of all the funds that the prosperity consciousness class would raise. The more people who attended, the higher my fee would be.

Another game! I said yes and quickly decided I was going to pack the room with people. I marketed the class to everyone I knew and everywhere I could think of. On the first day, I walked into the room and every chair was filled with many more people standing in the back. It was an awesome, high-energy class, and many people had breakthroughs.

After the class ended, when the organization's leader and I wrapped up the details, the amount of my fee came to exactly the amount that I had set as my goal. It didn't come in my timing, but it came at the exact right moment, in the exact right way. Life fulfilled its part of the contract by bringing the goal to me in exactly the right way (i.e., "how") and at the exact right time (i.e., "when").

I could easily have gotten discouraged or distracted. However, I knew I was working with a perfect law, which was working perfectly. My job was to fulfill my part of the Life Contract and let it all unfold.

We don't have to push and fight and manipulate to make Life work for us. In fact, the more we let Life do its part and just focus on our part, the more enjoyable and easy the process is.

The Third Side

If you look at the Life Contract Map (on page 2), which details how the Life Contract works, you'll notice that it shows a goal that we choose (top part of the triangle), our part of the Contract (lower left corner), and Life's part of the contract (lower right corner). We have discussed the forward movement that occurs when we take steps toward our goal (the up arrow on the left side), and how Life will mirror our effort (the up arrow on the right side).

You'll notice, however, that there is another side of the triangle we haven't talked about: the bottom that connects each of us with Life. On the map, you'll find an arrow pointing both directions under this link.

As we move toward our goal and as Life also moves toward our goal, that bottom of the triangle represents something very important: our communication with Life.

To revisit an example we discussed earlier, if I were in a contract with an architect to build my perfect house, and I fulfilled my part of the contractual requirements while the architect fulfilled his or hers, there is still one thing missing: communication. If I don't communicate with the architect about what kind of house I want and if the architect doesn't communicate what is needed from me, then how can my perfect house get built?

It's the same with Life. The more we communicate with Life, the more we are guided and directed by Life toward our goal. The less we communicate with Life, the less precise signals we are sending about what we want. If you truly want your goal, then communicating with Life is essential.

The question then becomes, how can you best communicate with Life?

There are many ways we can connect with Life. Traditional spiritual methods such as meditation and prayer are excellent places to start. (See the resources in part three for suggestions on books about meditation and prayer.) Sitting quietly in meditative silence while stilling your mind is a way to be quiet enough to "hear" your own soul's voice. Prayers of gratitude or asking for more direction can help give you strength and provide a clear channel.

There are two other methods that I have used with very good results. The first is journaling. I always keep a journal handy to write down thoughts, feelings, ideas, and anything else that seems important. When I'm stuck, I'll begin writing in my journal, and somehow I can write my way to more clarity. When I feel upset, I'll journal my way to the cause, and then write out a new outcome to the situation.

Journaling allows me to have a conversation with Life. I write down my thoughts, questions, concerns, gratitude lists, and everything else I can think of, and then I take a deep breath or two and let Life write back to me. I simply set my pen to the paper and begin to put down what my heart and my soul are telling me in that moment. I don't force it, and I don't consciously "make" anything happen. Some days very little comes through; other days pages will appear to almost write themselves. Either way, I can feel the truth of what is pouring out all the way down to the depths of my soul.

The second method is something called "Sitting for Ideas." I first discovered the original concept for this method in Napoleon Hill's book *Think and Grow Rich*. There, he told the story of an inventor describing his method of dreaming up new inventions. I loved that section of the book so much that I adapted it for my own use, and it has become one of the simplest and most powerful ways I connect to my soul. To read how to do it, go to the section called "Sitting for Ideas" in part three. You'll be able to begin using this tool immediately.

However you decide to generate more communication with Life, remember to connect at least once a day—or more often if possible. We have within ourselves a storehouse of knowledge, wisdom, and ideas always available to us and as close as our breath. By connecting to our inner wisdom daily, we are creating a conscious way to access our highest self. It's like always having the best life coach available to you at all times.

Now What?

We've gone over all the details of how the Life Contract works. Now it's time to put this information into practice in your life. After all, this is all theory until you begin to apply it and see results. It's time to get your life moving! Are you ready?

LIVING YOUR LIFE CONTRACT

What you hold in your hands might look like a small, simple book, but it is really a powerful tool of transformation. *My Life Contract* is a simple but effective way to prioritize goals and then record progress toward accomplishing them.

Part two of *My Life Contract* can keep you moving forward. As you do, hold your focus on your goals and action steps. Why is this important? When you do your part and concentrate on your actions, your part of the contract, you are creating a way for Life to do its part and help you.

As I mentioned earlier, I believe that Life wants more for us than we often want for ourselves. As we clarify our goals and then hold on to positive thoughts and take positive actions toward those goals, Life will see our commitment and match it.

Sometimes as you take daily steps toward your goals, you might notice ideas that come to you out of the blue, or a surprise e-mail or call from someone who wants to help you, or some other experience that we call a coincidence (or deny even happened). When you help yourself, you are opening the way for Life to lend a hand.

Using this Ninety-Day Goal Tracker has helped me accomplish many goals. My hope is that the Life Contract Ninety-Day Goal Tracker will be a part of your successful journey as well. Be creative, and make it your own. Utilize it in any way that will move you ahead. I look forward to hearing about your successes!

If You Don't Know What You Want, You'll Get Something Else

In the following pages you are going to be asked to do two main things: first, get clear about what you want, and second, take consistent actions toward that thing. While those might sound like simple tasks, they often turn out to be extremely difficult. Why? Some people don't know what goals or dreams to choose, which makes them tend not to choose anything. Result? No movement. Other people feel there are too many options and don't want to narrow it down to just a couple main goals, perhaps for fear of choosing the wrong things. Result? Again, no movement.

The answer is simply to *pick something* and move forward. If you don't know what you want, use the Possibilities section below to come up with ideas and narrow them down. You can also answer the Life Purpose Questionnaire in part three to generate some thoughts.

Don't get bogged down in whether you have picked something that is the ultimate, perfect goal or dream. For now, just reframe the goal and know that you are choosing something *for now*. Trust that it will lead you to the next thing which will be an even better fit if you just allow it. Just as any candle you ignite will generate enough light to see what is nearby, each goal you pick to ignite will generate enough light to show you the next steps, and then the next, and so on. Light your life by making a decision and following through.

Start Here

It's time. You are ready to move forward at last! Now what do you do?

I have asked myself that very question many times. A goal or a dream or an idea would come to mind, and then I would wonder what I should do next to accomplish that goal. In some cases, the goal would feel overwhelming or far away, and I would be paralyzed into nonaction.

But then I had a realization . . .

What if I took those big goals and divided them up into smaller, bite-sized goals? (And sometimes I would have to divide those goals into even smaller nibbles.) If I couldn't accomplish a big goal in one day or one week, I could at least take one step toward it. Eventually those steps add up. I would find myself moving toward my goal with surprising speed.

The key is consistency—working at the goal every single day.

To facilitate this, I created an early prototype of the journal section you find here: a daily notebook. The first thing I did was to write out my goal(s) in the front. Then, every morning, on one side of the page, I would write the steps that I wanted to accomplish that day. Every evening shortly before going to bed, I would use the other side of the page to put down what I actually did.

Some days I accomplished more than I had planned, and some days less. But over the course of ninety days, I noticed that, by and large, the notebook kept me on track and gave me a visual record of my progress. Seeing my journey laid out on paper motivated me to keep going. And when one ninety-day period ended, I would start another, and then another . . . until it became a way of life. Tracking progress toward goals works!

Now it's your turn.

Instructions

On the following pages, you will write down all the goals and dreams you have, and then be asked to prioritize no more than three. Any more than three, and you are not harnessing the full power of your energy effectively. You may find you only have one or two goals. You can use this journal just as effectively for that as well. You don't *need* to have three goals, but please don't have more than three.

Next, read the fine print about the Life Contract, and then—if you are committed—sign the contract.

In the following journaling pages, you'll see that each two-page spread covers one day. This is a simple method; it's important not to overcomplicate things.

On the left side of the spread, write down the steps you want to make toward your goal(s). Do this as early in your day as possible—right after you wake up if you can. Start your day focused on your priorities, which will help you be mindful of your goals and less inclined to get sidetracked throughout the day.

At the end of each day, write down on the right side of the spread all that you did that day toward your goals. If you didn't get much accomplished, use this realization to propel you into getting more accomplished tomorrow. Similarly, when you've accomplished all that you planned to do that day, stop there and rest.

Track this information every single day. If you happen to miss a day, don't let that stop you or sabotage your progress. Pick it right back up and start again. *Just keep moving!*

Time for the next step . . .

Possibilities

Below, make a list of your dreams, your goals, everything you want to accomplish. If you have clear ideas of what you want, put them down. If you don't, list those goals that you think would make you happy and bring you joy. Have fun with this list. Try to make it quickly, without overthinking. List as many things as you can in ten minutes or less, starting . . . NOW:

My Possibilities:

_____

_____

_____

_____

_____

_____

_____

_____

_____

_____

_____

_____

_____

_____

_____

_____

_____

_____

_____

_____

Narrow It Down

Choose the items on your possibilities list that you want to make a priority. Think about what you've written and begin to narrow it down. Circle or put a star next to those goals that make you the happiest, that feel the most "you." Once you have clarified for yourself which items on the list are the ones you want to focus on, use the spaces here to write out your top three priorities, and then the goals you'll want to accomplish after those top three priorities are accomplished.

My Top Three Priorities:

_____
_____
_____
_____
_____
_____
_____
_____
_____

What I'll Do Next:

_____
_____
_____
_____
_____
_____
_____
_____
_____

My Three Goals

Now put each of your top three goals in one present-tense sentence. On the next line, explain it in more detail, adding descriptive words so that the goal comes alive. Finally, write down how you will feel when the goal actually comes true for you. By adding the feeling, you are doing what Napoleon Hill calls "building a stronger fire"—making your goals more urgent and exciting.

Goal #1:

_____

Describe it fully:

_____

_____

_____

What it will feel like when I accomplish this goal:

_____

_____

_____

Goal #2:

_____

Describe it fully:

_____

_____

_____

What it will feel like when I accomplish this goal:

_____

_____

_____

Goal #3:

_____

Describe it fully:

_____

_____

_____

What it will feel like when I accomplish this goal:

_____

_____

_____

The Fine Print

As discussed in part one, now that you know what you want, you need to make a decision. This decision represents your commitment to yourself and to Life. It's helpful to create a contract as a physical representation of your commitment. Before filling out the Life Contract on the next page, look at the statements below and check each one that you will agree to over the next ninety days:

- ☐ I will do what it takes, and spend time each day on these three goals.

- ☐ If by chance I miss a day, I will pick right back up and keep going.

- ☐ I will maintain a positive attitude, and will be a positive force in the world.

- ☐ I won't let discouragement, negativity, the past, anyone, or anything stop me.

- ☐ I know that fulfilling my goals will better my life and the world around me.

☐ My actions will speak louder than any words.

☐ If I finish early, I will choose another goal.

☐ If I don't finish in ninety days, I will keep going until I do.

☐ No excuses.

If you checked most (or hopefully all) of the statements above, you are ready make your commitment and move forward. Fill out the Contract with Life, and then begin your journey . . .

My Life Contract

I, _____, now commit to myself,
and to Life, for the next ninety days, starting today,
to follow through on the following three goals:

Goal #1: _____

Goal #2: _____

Goal #3: _____

I'm ready.
Now is the time.
No more waiting.
Nothing can stop me now.

Signed: _____

Today's Date: _____

Ninety Days from Now: _____

THE LIFE CONTRACT NINETY-DAY GOAL TRACKER

My Plan for Today – Day 1

Today I Will . . .

GOAL #1:

GOAL #2:

GOAL #3:

Today's Results:

GOAL #1:

GOAL #2:

GOAL #3:

My Plan for Today – Day 2

Today I Will . . .

GOAL #1:

GOAL #2:

GOAL #3:

Today's Results:

GOAL #1:

GOAL #2:

GOAL #3:

My Plan for Today – Day 3

Today I Will . . .

GOAL #1:

GOAL #2:

GOAL #3:

Today's Results:

GOAL #1:

GOAL #2:

GOAL #3:

My Plan for Today – Day 4

Today I Will . . .

GOAL #1:

GOAL #2:

GOAL #3:

Today's Results:

GOAL #1:

GOAL #2:

GOAL #3:

My Plan for Today – Day 5

Today I Will . . .

GOAL #1:

GOAL #2:

GOAL #3:

Today's Results:

GOAL #1:

GOAL #2:

GOAL #3:

My Plan for Today – Day 6

Today I Will . . .

GOAL #1:

GOAL #2:

GOAL #3:

Today's Results:

GOAL #1:

GOAL #2:

GOAL #3:

My Plan for Today – Day 7

Today I Will . . .

GOAL #1:

GOAL #2:

GOAL #3:

Today's Results:

GOAL #1:

GOAL #2:

GOAL #3:

My Plan for Today – Day 8

Today I Will . . .

GOAL #1:

GOAL #2:

GOAL #3:

Today's Results:

GOAL #1:

GOAL #2:

GOAL #3:

My Plan for Today – Day 9

Today I Will . . .

GOAL #1:

GOAL #2:

GOAL #3:

Today's Results:

GOAL #1:

GOAL #2:

GOAL #3:

My Plan for Today – Day 10

Today I Will . . .

GOAL #1:

GOAL #2:

GOAL #3:

Today's Results:

GOAL #1:

GOAL #2:

GOAL #3:

My Plan for Today – Day 11

Today I Will . . .

GOAL #1:

GOAL #2:

GOAL #3:

Today's Results:

GOAL #1:

GOAL #2:

GOAL #3:

My Plan for Today – Day 12

Today I Will . . .

GOAL #1:

GOAL #2:

GOAL #3:

Today's Results:

GOAL #1:

GOAL #2:

GOAL #3:

My Plan for Today – Day 13

Today I Will . . .

GOAL #1:

GOAL #2:

GOAL #3:

Today's Results:

GOAL #1:

GOAL #2:

GOAL #3:

My Plan for Today – Day 14

Today I Will . . .

GOAL #1:

GOAL #2:

GOAL #3:

Today's Results:

GOAL #1:

GOAL #2:

GOAL #3:

My Plan for Today – Day 15

Today I Will . . .

GOAL #1:

GOAL #2:

GOAL #3:

Today's Results:

GOAL #1:

GOAL #2:

GOAL #3:

My Plan for Today – Day 16

Today I Will . . .

GOAL #1:

GOAL #2:

GOAL #3:

Today's Results:

GOAL #1:

GOAL #2:

GOAL #3:

My Plan for Today – Day 17

Today I Will . . .

GOAL #1:

GOAL #2:

GOAL #3:

Today's Results:

GOAL #1:

GOAL #2:

GOAL #3:

My Plan for Today – Day 18

Today I Will . . .

GOAL #1:

GOAL #2:

GOAL #3:

Today's Results:

GOAL #1:

GOAL #2:

GOAL #3:

My Plan for Today – Day 19

Today I Will . . .

GOAL #1:

GOAL #2:

GOAL #3:

Today's Results:

GOAL #1:

GOAL #2:

GOAL #3:

My Plan for Today – Day 20

Today I Will . . .

GOAL #1:

GOAL #2:

GOAL #3:

Today's Results:

GOAL #1:

GOAL #2:

GOAL #3:

My Plan for Today – Day 21

Today I Will . . .

GOAL #1:

GOAL #2:

GOAL #3:

Today's Results:

GOAL #1:

GOAL #2:

GOAL #3:

My Plan for Today – Day 22

Today I Will . . .

GOAL #1:

GOAL #2:

GOAL #3:

Today's Results:

GOAL #1:

GOAL #2:

GOAL #3:

My Plan for Today – Day 23

Today I Will . . .

GOAL #1:

GOAL #2:

GOAL #3:

Today's Results:

GOAL #1:

GOAL #2:

GOAL #3:

My Plan for Today – Day 24

Today I Will . . .

GOAL #1:

GOAL #2:

GOAL #3:

Today's Results:

GOAL #1:

GOAL #2:

GOAL #3:

My Plan for Today – Day 25

Today I Will . . .

GOAL #1:

GOAL #2:

GOAL #3:

Today's Results:

GOAL #1:

GOAL #2:

GOAL #3:

My Plan for Today – Day 26

Today I Will . . .

GOAL #1:

GOAL #2:

GOAL #3:

Today's Results:

GOAL #1:

GOAL #2:

GOAL #3:

My Plan for Today – Day 27

Today I Will . . .

GOAL #1:

GOAL #2:

GOAL #3:

Today's Results:

GOAL #1:

GOAL #2:

GOAL #3:

My Plan for Today – Day 28

Today I Will . . .

GOAL #1:

GOAL #2:

GOAL #3:

Today's Results:

GOAL #1:

GOAL #2:

GOAL #3:

My Plan for Today – Day 29

Today I Will . . .

GOAL #1:

GOAL #2:

GOAL #3:

Today's Results:

GOAL #1:

GOAL #2:

GOAL #3:

My Plan for Today – Day 30

Today I Will . . .

GOAL #1:

GOAL #2:

GOAL #3:

Today's Results:

GOAL #1:

GOAL #2:

GOAL #3:

My Plan for Today – Day 31

Today I Will . . .

GOAL #1:

GOAL #2:

GOAL #3:

Today's Results:

GOAL #1:

GOAL #2:

GOAL #3:

My Plan for Today – Day 32

Today I Will . . .

GOAL #1:

GOAL #2:

GOAL #3:

Today's Results:

GOAL #1:

GOAL #2:

GOAL #3:

My Plan for Today – Day 33

Today I Will . . .

GOAL #1:

GOAL #2:

GOAL #3:

Today's Results:

GOAL #1:

GOAL #2:

GOAL #3:

My Plan for Today – Day 34

Today I Will . . .

GOAL #1:

GOAL #2:

GOAL #3:

Today's Results:

GOAL #1:

GOAL #2:

GOAL #3:

My Plan for Today – Day 35

Today I Will . . .

GOAL #1:

GOAL #2:

GOAL #3:

Today's Results:

GOAL #1:

GOAL #2:

GOAL #3:

My Plan for Today – Day 36

Today I Will . . .

GOAL #1:

GOAL #2:

GOAL #3:

Today's Results:

GOAL #1:

GOAL #2:

GOAL #3:

My Plan for Today – Day 37

Today I Will . . .

GOAL #1:

GOAL #2:

GOAL #3:

Today's Results:

GOAL #1:

GOAL #2:

GOAL #3:

My Plan for Today – Day 38

Today I Will . . .

GOAL #1:

GOAL #2:

GOAL #3:

Today's Results:

GOAL #1:

GOAL #2:

GOAL #3:

My Plan for Today – Day 39

Today I Will . . .

GOAL #1:

GOAL #2:

GOAL #3:

Today's Results:

GOAL #1:

GOAL #2:

GOAL #3:

My Plan for Today – Day 40

Today I Will . . .

GOAL #1:

GOAL #2:

GOAL #3:

Today's Results:

GOAL #1:

GOAL #2:

GOAL #3:

My Plan for Today – Day 41

Today I Will . . .

GOAL #1:

GOAL #2:

GOAL #3:

Today's Results:

GOAL #1:

GOAL #2:

GOAL #3:

My Plan for Today – Day 42

Today I Will . . .

GOAL #1:

GOAL #2:

GOAL #3:

Today's Results:

GOAL #1:

GOAL #2:

GOAL #3:

My Plan for Today – Day 43

Today I Will . . .

GOAL #1:

GOAL #2:

GOAL #3:

Today's Results:

GOAL #1:

GOAL #2:

GOAL #3:

My Plan for Today – Day 44

Today I Will . . .

GOAL #1:

GOAL #2:

GOAL #3:

Today's Results:

GOAL #1:

GOAL #2:

GOAL #3:

My Plan for Today – Day 45

Today I Will . . .

GOAL #1:

GOAL #2:

GOAL #3:

Today's Results:

GOAL #1:

GOAL #2:

GOAL #3:

My Plan for Today – Day 46

Today I Will . . .

GOAL #1:

GOAL #2:

GOAL #3:

Today's Results:

GOAL #1:

GOAL #2:

GOAL #3:

My Plan for Today – Day 47

Today I Will . . .

GOAL #1:

GOAL #2:

GOAL #3:

Today's Results:

GOAL #1:

GOAL #2:

GOAL #3:

My Plan for Today – Day 48

Today I Will . . .

GOAL #1:

GOAL #2:

GOAL #3:

Today's Results:

GOAL #1:

GOAL #2:

GOAL #3:

My Plan for Today – Day 49

Today I Will . . .

GOAL #1:

GOAL #2:

GOAL #3:

Today's Results:

GOAL #1:

GOAL #2:

GOAL #3:

My Plan for Today – Day 50

Today I Will . . .

GOAL #1:

GOAL #2:

GOAL #3:

Today's Results:

GOAL #1:

GOAL #2:

GOAL #3:

My Plan for Today – Day 51

Today I Will . . .

GOAL #1:

GOAL #2:

GOAL #3:

Today's Results:

GOAL #1:

GOAL #2:

GOAL #3:

My Plan for Today – Day 52

Today I Will . . .

GOAL #1:

GOAL #2:

GOAL #3:

Today's Results:

GOAL #1:

GOAL #2:

GOAL #3:

My Plan for Today – Day 53

Today I Will . . .

GOAL #1:

GOAL #2:

GOAL #3:

Today's Results:

GOAL #1:

GOAL #2:

GOAL #3:

My Plan for Today – Day 54

Today I Will . . .

GOAL #1:

GOAL #2:

GOAL #3:

Today's Results:

GOAL #1:

GOAL #2:

GOAL #3:

My Plan for Today – Day 55

Today I Will . . .

GOAL #1:

GOAL #2:

GOAL #3:

Today's Results:

GOAL #1:

GOAL #2:

GOAL #3:

My Plan for Today – Day 56

Today I Will . . .

GOAL #1:

GOAL #2:

GOAL #3:

Today's Results:

GOAL #1:

GOAL #2:

GOAL #3:

My Plan for Today – Day 57

Today I Will . . .

GOAL #1:

GOAL #2:

GOAL #3:

Today's Results:

GOAL #1:

GOAL #2:

GOAL #3:

My Plan for Today – Day 58

Today I Will . . .

GOAL #1:

GOAL #2:

GOAL #3:

Today's Results:

GOAL #1:

GOAL #2:

GOAL #3:

My Plan for Today – Day 59

Today I Will . . .

GOAL #1:

GOAL #2:

GOAL #3:

Today's Results:

GOAL #1:

GOAL #2:

GOAL #3:

My Plan for Today – Day 60

Today I Will . . .

GOAL #1:

GOAL #2:

GOAL #3:

Today's Results:

GOAL #1:

GOAL #2:

GOAL #3:

My Plan for Today – Day 61

Today I Will . . .

GOAL #1:

GOAL #2:

GOAL #3:

Today's Results:

GOAL #1:

GOAL #2:

GOAL #3:

My Plan for Today – Day 62

Today I Will . . .

GOAL #1:

GOAL #2:

GOAL #3:

Today's Results:

GOAL #1:

GOAL #2:

GOAL #3:

My Plan for Today – Day 63

Today I Will . . .

GOAL #1:

GOAL #2:

GOAL #3:

Today's Results:

GOAL #1:

GOAL #2:

GOAL #3:

My Plan for Today – Day 64

Today I Will . . .

GOAL #1:

GOAL #2:

GOAL #3:

Today's Results:

GOAL #1:

GOAL #2:

GOAL #3:

My Plan for Today – Day 65

Today I Will . . .

GOAL #1:

GOAL #2:

GOAL #3:

Today's Results:

GOAL #1:

GOAL #2:

GOAL #3:

My Plan for Today – Day 66

Today I Will . . .

GOAL #1:

GOAL #2:

GOAL #3:

Today's Results:

GOAL #1:

GOAL #2:

GOAL #3:

My Plan for Today – Day 67

Today I Will . . .

GOAL #1:

GOAL #2:

GOAL #3:

Today's Results:

GOAL #1:

GOAL #2:

GOAL #3:

My Plan for Today – Day 68

Today I Will . . .

GOAL #1:

GOAL #2:

GOAL #3:

Today's Results:

GOAL #1:

GOAL #2:

GOAL #3:

My Plan for Today – Day 69

Today I Will . . .

GOAL #1:

GOAL #2:

GOAL #3:

Today's Results:

GOAL #1:

GOAL #2:

GOAL #3:

My Plan for Today – Day 70

Today I Will . . .

GOAL #1:

GOAL #2:

GOAL #3:

Today's Results:

GOAL #1:

GOAL #2:

GOAL #3:

My Plan for Today – Day 71

Today I Will . . .

GOAL #1:

GOAL #2:

GOAL #3:

Today's Results:

GOAL #1:

GOAL #2:

GOAL #3:

My Plan for Today – Day 72

Today I Will . . .

GOAL #1:

GOAL #2:

GOAL #3:

Today's Results:

GOAL #1:

GOAL #2:

GOAL #3:

My Plan for Today – Day 73

Today I Will . . .

GOAL #1:

GOAL #2:

GOAL #3:

Today's Results:

GOAL #1:

GOAL #2:

GOAL #3:

My Plan for Today – Day 74

Today I Will . . .

GOAL #1:

GOAL #2:

GOAL #3:

Today's Results:

GOAL #1:

GOAL #2:

GOAL #3:

My Plan for Today – Day 75

Today I Will . . .

GOAL #1:

GOAL #2:

GOAL #3:

Today's Results:

GOAL #1:

GOAL #2:

GOAL #3:

My Plan for Today – Day 76

Today I Will . . .

GOAL #1:

GOAL #2:

GOAL #3:

Today's Results:

GOAL #1:

GOAL #2:

GOAL #3:

My Plan for Today – Day 77

Today I Will . . .

GOAL #1:

GOAL #2:

GOAL #3:

Today's Results:

GOAL #1:

GOAL #2:

GOAL #3:

My Plan for Today – Day 78

Today I Will . . .

GOAL #1:

GOAL #2:

GOAL #3:

Today's Results:

GOAL #1:

GOAL #2:

GOAL #3:

My Plan for Today – Day 79

Today I Will . . .

GOAL #1:

GOAL #2:

GOAL #3:

Today's Results:

GOAL #1:

GOAL #2:

GOAL #3:

My Plan for Today – Day 80

Today I Will . . .

GOAL #1:

GOAL #2:

GOAL #3:

Today's Results:

GOAL #1:

GOAL #2:

GOAL #3:

My Plan for Today – Day 81

Today I Will . . .

GOAL #1:

GOAL #2:

GOAL #3:

Today's Results:

GOAL #1:

GOAL #2:

GOAL #3:

My Plan for Today – Day 82

Today I Will . . .

GOAL #1:

GOAL #2:

GOAL #3:

Today's Results:

GOAL #1:

GOAL #2:

GOAL #3:

My Plan for Today – Day 83

Today I Will . . .

GOAL #1:

GOAL #2:

GOAL #3:

Today's Results:

GOAL #1:

GOAL #2:

GOAL #3:

My Plan for Today – Day 84

Today I Will . . .

GOAL #1:

GOAL #2:

GOAL #3:

Today's Results:

GOAL #1:

GOAL #2:

GOAL #3:

My Plan for Today – Day 85

Today I Will . . .

GOAL #1:

GOAL #2:

GOAL #3:

Today's Results:

GOAL #1:

GOAL #2:

GOAL #3:

My Plan for Today – Day 86

Today I Will . . .

GOAL #1:

GOAL #2:

GOAL #3:

Today's Results:

GOAL #1:

GOAL #2:

GOAL #3:

My Plan for Today – Day 87

Today I Will . . .

GOAL #1:

GOAL #2:

GOAL #3:

Today's Results:

GOAL #1:

GOAL #2:

GOAL #3:

My Plan for Today – Day 88

Today I Will . . .

GOAL #1:

GOAL #2:

GOAL #3:

Today's Results:

GOAL #1:

GOAL #2:

GOAL #3:

My Plan for Today – Day 89

Today I Will . . .

GOAL #1:

GOAL #2:

GOAL #3:

Today's Results:

GOAL #1:

GOAL #2:

GOAL #3:

My Plan for Today – Day 90

Today I Will . . .

GOAL #1:

GOAL #2:

GOAL #3:

Today's Results:

GOAL #1:

GOAL #2:

GOAL #3:

CONGRATULATIONS

You did it! You finished your ninety-day journey toward your dreams.

You've just done what most people don't—taking consistent steps forward and staying with it. You've created momentum, dealt with roadblocks, and kept moving even on the days that you probably felt like giving up. You inspire us all!

Yes, you may not have done it perfectly—you may have missed a day or two, there may have been a couple days you could have done more—but perfect is *not* the goal.

- Consistency is the goal.

- Creating positive habits is the goal.

- Putting your dreams first in your life is the goal.

And you are doing just that.

Take a bow. Pat yourself on the back. Allow yourself some time to feel good.

And now ask yourself . . .

What's Next?

Write down what you learned over the last ninety days. What are you proud of? What could you have done better? What will you do next time? Did you achieve your goals? If you did, what are your next goals? If not, how will you keep moving forward? It's never too soon to make a plan!

PART THREE

LIFE CONTRACT RESOURCES

Life Purpose Questionnaire

I've found that many people have no idea what they want to do with their life. They either feel overwhelmed with possibilities and don't know where to start, or they feel like there is nothing specific that is calling to them. Either way, they are stuck where they are.

I developed these questions over the years, adding some things and taking others away, depending on what works. The list now represents those questions that have had the greatest impact on the people I've worked with in the last twenty-plus years.

Remember: sometimes the simplest questions yield the most profound results.

I remember giving these questions to a group in a workshop a few years ago, and one of the participants raised his hand with the query, "Don't you have more challenging questions?" He was fooled by the simplicity and familiarity of what was being asked. I replied that these seemingly easy questions are the ones that appear to unlock our hearts and let our dreams come to the surface.

The key *is* the simplicity. The more seriously we take the question, the more profound our answer will be. That man who raised his hand did the questionnaire and ended up having a revelation that resulted in him following a brand-new path.

Read through these questions one at a time and have your journal handy. Write down whatever answers come. Don't judge as you write, and don't try to answer the questions "correctly." Just respond to them from your heart, without overthinking them. You can work through the whole questionnaire in one sitting, or you can do one a day and see how your answers evolve.

Remember:

- Don't overthink it.

- Don't be limited by what you can see or scenarios you create.

- Chances are that the way it turns out will be different than you imagine.

- You may have considered some of these questions before, but keep an open mind and think about them again.

- Use your journal to record your answers.

- Don't force it, and don't judge.

1. If you could do anything for a career, what would you do?

Why this is important: The dreams you have, starting with those dreams you had as a child, are guides that keep you moving forward. Even if a dream feels unattainable, it can be a compass to give you a direction.

2. Name three (or more) people who have careers that you admire and would like to emulate.

Why this is important: We are drawn to certain people for a reason—they represent something that we want to awaken and pursue in our own life.

3. What do you currently do that drains you? What energizes you?

Why this is important: Our feelings are clues to our life purpose. When you do something and feel drained afterward, this is an indicator you are going in the wrong direction. When you do something and feel energized by it, you know you are going in the right direction.

4. What would you do if money weren't an issue?

Why this is important: We often delay our dreams by saying that we will get started once we have more money. We think of money as security, rather than realizing that we are using money as an excuse not to live the life we love.

5. What would you do if you knew you could not fail?

Why this is important: This is a variation on the question above, but with a different emphasis. We often want guarantees from life that we won't fail before we move forward. In my opinion, staying stuck is a bigger risk than trying something and failing. Every so-called "failure" is actually a stepping-stone to success.

6. What do those closest to you say are your gifts or talents? What would your best friend say is the perfect career for you? (If you don't know, ask them!)

Why this is important: I've discovered that friends and family can often spot patterns in our own lives that we can't always see for ourselves. It's valuable to get their feedback and find out if they have any ideas that surprise and perhaps excite you.

7. What hobbies or interests do you have that you think would never be income-producing?

Why this is important: Many, many people over the years have told me that they could never make money doing what they love. One person told me she could never make any money designing fabric because she didn't have any training. However, after the workshop she decided to pursue it anyway. When she stuck with her Life Contract, things happened, and long story short, she now makes good money designing fabric. Why not you?

8. Do you feel you are more creative/right-brained or more analytical/left-brained? Or a good combination of the two? Do you tend to work better by yourself or with others? Are you a lone wolf or a team player?

Why this is important: These questions narrow down not only what you could do in your life, but how you could do it. Knowledge is power, and knowing your tendencies and how you work can help you design the perfect career.

9. List ten common careers that you are sure are *not* for you. What do they have in common? What would be the opposite of those careers?

Why this is important: When people tell me they have no idea what they *want* to do, I find they usually have very definite ideas of what they *don't want* and why. Knowing what you don't want helps you get closer to what you do want.

10. What would be your perfect setting, salary, hours, and environment for a career?

Why this is important: This is another way at getting to what you would like. Some people cannot tell me what career they want, but they are able to gain insights when I ask them to describe the details of what a perfect job might include.

11. If you could design a perfect job based on what you like to do, what might that job include?

Why this is important: As with #10, this question asks you to not think about what you could do or what you should do or what has worked for you in the past, but rather what you would like in a career.

12. Get a newspaper and read through the articles for clues. Every time you come across an article that lists someone doing something that you think would be fulfilling, fun, and/or interesting circle the article, or the part of the article, that caught your interest. Make a list of what you circled. What conclusions can you draw?

Why this is important: Using newspapers is a good way to get exposed to many different ideas, careers, and possibilities that you might not think of by yourself.

13. Would the perfect career involve any of the following (check all the ones that appeal to you):

☐ children ☐ food ☐ computers ☐ art ☐ designing ☐ management
☐ meetings ☐ teaching ☐ spirituality ☐ math/accounting
☐ helping others ☐ health/wellness ☐ working in an office
☐ working at home ☐ normal hours ☐ unusual hours ☐ writing
☐ building ☐ sales ☐ interacting with others ☐ travel ☐ other_____

Make a list of those you checked and elaborate how each would fit a need or want you would have in a career.

Why this is important: These descriptions are prompts that might spark ideas and help you narrow down what feels right.

14. What legacy would you like to leave behind? How would you like to make your mark in the world?

Why this is important: This is a way of "working backward." By thinking about how you would like your legacy to look, you can see what you need to do now to make sure that legacy comes true.

15. If someone offered you one million dollars to do a job of your choice for one year, what jobs come to mind?

Why this is important: This question takes away two of the fears that many people have: the fear of not having enough money and the fear of being locked in a career they don't love. If you remove both of those fears in your imagination, what does that open up for you?

16. Do this exercise: Take a deep breath and close your eyes. When your eyes are closed, ask yourself: "What does Life want me to do? What would I like to do? What's next for me?" Sit for a few moments and let ideas come to mind—don't force, don't judge—and when you are done, write down anything that turned up. Try doing this every day for a week. If nothing comes up, don't stress, and try it again tomorrow.

Why this is important: This question calls for you to relax and not force any answers. When we relax, we are open to hearing what our soul would love for us to do.

17. If you can't think of a career that would be a perfect fit, what careers might be good fits—or pretty good fits? What would it take to make those almost-perfect careers into ones that would be joyous and fulfilling? (*NOTE:* Don't use the word "perfect.")

Why this is important: It's easy to get hung up on finding that "perfect" job or career. So let's take the word "perfect" out of the equation, and think about what might be a "good" job—something you would like to do without the pressure of making it perfect.

18. Do any of your friends or family members have a career that you would like to try? What is it, and could you ask them questions about it?
Why this is important: Sometimes we see a close friend or family member in a career that appeals to us. Why not ask them more about it and see if it might be something that would be good for you as well? It might be nice to have a loved one share the same career as you!

Sitting for Ideas

This is a powerful tool for discovery and connection with Life. I use it every day. It comes from Napoleon Hill's success classic *Think and Grow Rich*, where Hill describes how one inventor used a process of sitting alone in a room with low lighting and a pad and pencil. In the silence, he came up with ideas for new inventions and solutions to problems with his inventions.

I loved this story so much, I simplified and adapted the process into something that I could use in my life. Here's what I do:

1. I find a quiet place where I can sit comfortably for at least ten minutes without being disturbed.

2. I make sure to have a notebook and a pen, and I put them next to me.

3. I close my eyes, take a few deep breaths, and then ask a question: *Life, what would you have me do today?* (You can ask any question, it doesn't have to be this one.)

4. I slowly repeat that question over and over again. As I repeat the question, different thoughts and ideas flash in my mind. Each time an idea of something for me to do shows up, I

write it down in my notebook, without judgment. I repeat this process for at least ten minutes.

5. When I'm done, I look at the "answers" I wrote down, and then I set out to do them. I try to do them the same day that I write them down.

That's it. It's amazing that something so transformative can be so simple! The key is to do it consistently, not hurry the process, and to write down anything that comes up. Some days I'll have a long list of things that come to mind, and other days it'll just be one or two. Sometimes what I write down makes sense, and sometimes what I write down only makes sense later after I do it.

For instance, one time as I was Sitting for Ideas, I had the thought "call Blair." I hadn't communicated with my old friend Blair for years, but since it popped up during my sitting, I wrote it down without thinking too much about it. Later, when I looked at my list from that day, I wondered why Blair's name had come to mind, and then I wondered whatever had happened to her.

Using social media, I was able to find Blair easily and send her a quick e-mail. About three minutes after it went out, I got a reply saying, "OMG, I was just thinking about you. I've got a new business, and I wanted to hire you to come and speak to a group of employees, but I didn't know how to get a hold of you."

If I had ignored that prompting, I might not have reconnected with Blair, and she might not have decided to take the extra steps to find me. But I didn't ignore the prompting, and not only did I get a speaking job from it, I also reconnected with an old friend.

Try Sitting for Ideas for yourself, and see what positive activities and ideas come through to you. Use this tool every morning as you fill out your Life Contract daily goal tracker when deciding what to do for each of your goals.

Creating a Master Mind

One of the best ways to stay the course and complete your Life Contract is to create a Master Mind partnership or group. You do not have to walk this journey by yourself.

Working with a Master Mind partner or a Master Mind group is a great way to connect with like-minded people whom we can support and get support from. Studies show that when we embark on a journey with a friend or support person, we are more likely to achieve our goal than if we do it by ourselves. I can add from years of experience, it's also a lot more fun!

I have more complete instructions for forming a Master Mind partnership or Master Mind group in my book *The Think and Grow Rich Journey*, but here are some general guidelines that should get you started:

Master Mind partner or Master Mind group?

A *Master Mind* is two or more people coming together to provide support, inspiration, and accountability for the goals of each member. Master Mind partners are you and one other person, and a Master Mind group is three or more people.

Do you work better in one-on-one settings? Or with a group? Either a partner or group can be beneficial, so choose the one that calls to you the most. You can always change it as you go on.

Choosing Partner(s):

- Make sure to pick people who have the same level of commitment to their Life Contract as you do to yours. It's important to have a peer, not someone you have to cajole or force.

- Also, make sure to choose people who will communicate with you in an honest yet compassionate way. Do not choose people who are lukewarm or who are only focused on themselves and not interested in your journey.

- Pick people who are open to learning, who are positive, and who are excited about their Life Contract. You don't need negativity in your life.

- Think outside the box when deciding whom to choose. It might be easier to pick a spouse, a close friend, or a family member, but are those the right choice? Sometimes it works better to find someone you don't know as well, as they won't have any preconceived notions about you and what you should be doing.

- Look for potential people at your job, your church, within your social circle, or even in those places where you do your hobby or side interest (craft, sports, shared interests).

Meet Consistently:

- Once you find the right person(s), make a commitment to meet weekly for at least one hour. Give each person an equal amount of time to speak and discuss their Life Contract experiences.

- Meeting in person is preferable. Places you can meet include someone's home (with no distractions!), library meeting rooms, nonprofit organizations you are connected to, or a restaurant. You could even meet outside, weather permitting.

- If meeting in person is impossible, you can also use modern technology (phone, Skype, etc.).

- Try to not cancel meetings. The more you make your meetings a priority, the more powerful they will be for you.

Tips for Good Meetings:

- Choose people with whom you feel a creative energy and who will engage with you as much as you engage with them. It's no fun studying with someone who only talks about themselves and doesn't ask questions of the other person.

- Give each person a set period of time to talk about how the ideas in the book relate to their life. When the time is up, move to the next person. When one person dominates, the group experience is lessened.

- If a Master Mind partner or group member is doing something that you don't like—such as not spending as much time supporting you as you do them—then tell them. Don't hold in the negative feelings or gossip about it to someone else. Just explain what you need (i.e., more interest or energy from them, etc.). If they want to continue, great. If they don't, then part as friends as quickly as possible and find someone new to work with.

- This book includes the Ninety-Day Goal Tracker, which is approximately thirteen weeks or just over three months. Make a commitment to meet once a week for the duration of the thirteen weeks.

- At the end of the thirteen weeks, reward yourselves with a celebratory meal or toast your accomplishment.

- Also at the end of the thirteen weeks, review together what worked, what didn't work, and then decide how you want to move forward for the next thirteen weeks. If you don't want to work with the same people again, shake hands as friends and wish one another well. Then, look for new people to share your next ninety-day process.

FURTHER READING

It is especially important to read inspirational books (or listen to inspirational audiobooks) as you fulfill your Life Contract. The following are recommendations to keep you motivated and focused during your Life Contract experience.

Check them off one at a time as you read them:

☐ *Think and Grow Rich: The Master Mind Volume* – Napoleon Hill

☐ *Think and Grow Rich Every Day: 365 Days of Success* – Napoleon Hill with Joel Fotinos and August Gold

☐ *The Think and Grow Rich Journey: Enhance and Enrich Your Path to Success* – Joel Fotinos

☐ *The Power of Decision : A Step-by-Step Program to Overcome Indecision and Live Freely Forever* – Raymond Charles Barker

☐ *The Science of Getting Rich* – Wallace D. Wattles

☐ *The Game of Life & How to Play It* – Florence Scovel Shinn

☐ *The Magic of Thinking Big* – David J. Schwartz

☐ *Now What?: 90 Days to a New Life Direction* – Laura Berman Fortgang

☐ *Inspired & Unstoppable: Wildly Succeeding in Your Life's Work!* – Tama Kieves

☐ *The Million Dollar Secret Hidden in Your Mind* – Anthony Norvell

☐ *The Now Habit : A Strategic Program for Overcoming Procrastination and Enjoying Guilt-Free Play* – Neil Fiore

☐ *The Optimist Creed* – Christian D. Larson

☐ *The Big Leap : Conquer Your Hidden Fear and Take Life to the Next Level* – Gay Hendricks

☐ *The Magic of Believing* – Claude M. Bristol

☐ *Meditation : An In-Depth Guide* – Ian Gawler and Paul Bedson

☐ *The Art of Uncertainty: How to Live in the Mystery of Life and Love It* – Dennis Merritt Jones

INSPIRING WORDS

Here is the great secret ... you will realize your ideal when you become exactly like your ideal, and you will realize as much of your ideal now as you develop in yourself now.
—Christian Larson

One of the most common causes of failure is the habit of quitting when one is overtaken by temporary defeat.
—Napoleon Hill

Indecision is actually the individual's decision to fail.
—Raymond Charles Barker

Do not wait for a change of environment before you act; get a change of environment by action.
—Wallace D. Wattles

Write in other quotes that inspire you:

ACKNOWLEDGMENTS

Many thanks to Greg Brandenburgh, and everyone at Hampton Roads Publishing Company. Also many thanks to Laura Berman Fortgang for her introduction and friendship. Great gratitude goes to August Gold, my creative partner of more than a dozen years (and counting). My gratitude also to those friends, supporters, colleagues, and cheerleaders along the way, including (but not limited to) Tama Kieves, Michelle Wadleigh, Chris Michaels, Mary Kay Carney, Julia Cameron, Lisa & David Gamble, Pat Stephenson, Denise Silvestro, Mitch Horowitz, Lynn Garrett, and everyone at the Center for Spiritual Living North Jersey. And especially, my love and thanks to Team Family—Alan Stephenson, Raphi Fotinos Stephenson, Cheryle Robinson, and my wonderful mother K. Lorraine Fotinos.

ABOUT THE AUTHOR

Photo by Carl Studna

Joel Fotinos, known as the *Spiritual Businessman,* is a vice president at Penguin Random House and publisher of the Tarcher/Penguin imprint. He is the coauthor of *The Prayer Chest*, which Judy Collins called "a wonderful and enlightening book." The book was a Family Circle Book of the Month, as well as endorsed by Christiane Northrup, MD, Julia Cameron, Catherine Ponder, and many others. Fotinos has also written or cowritten several other books, including *Multiply Your Blessings*, *A Little Daily Wisdom*, and *The Think and Grow Rich Workbook*. His books have over 120,000 copies in print and have been published in fourteen languages. Fotinos has been featured in many magazines and newspapers and was given *Science of Mind* magazine's first "Outstanding Individual of the Year" award.

A licensed minister with the Centers for Spiritual Living, Fotinos travels the country giving talks and workshops on spirituality and inspiration. He also speaks once a month and gives ongoing classes in northern New Jersey. Fotinos has narrated many audiobooks, including the nationally best-selling audio editions for Napoleon Hill's *Think and Grow Rich* and *The Law of Success*. He is the male voice for Penguin Classics' "Poems By Heart," which has been downloaded over 300,000 times, and "Bible Verses By Heart" apps. He lives with his family in New Jersey.

www.joelfotinos.com
Facebook: /joelfotinos1
Twitter: @joelfotinos

Hampton Roads Publishing Company

...for the evolving human spirit

Hampton Roads Publishing Company publishes books on a variety of subjects, including spirituality, health, and other related topics.

For a copy of our latest trade catalog, call (978) 465-0504 or visit our distributor's website at *www.redwheelweiser.com*. You can also sign up for our newsletter and special offers by going to *www.redwheelweiser.com/newsletter/*.